African
HEROES

DISCOVERING OUR
CHRISTIAN HERITAGE

Jerome Gay Jr.
ILLUSTRATED BY JOHN JOVEN

New Growth Press, Greensboro, NC 27401
Copyright ©2023 Jerome Gay Jr.

Cover/Interior illustrations: John Joven
Design/Typesetting: Dan Stelzer

ISBN: 978-1-64507-263-8

Library of Congress Cataloging-in-Publication Data on file
Printed in India
30 29 28 27 26 25 24 23   1 2 3 4 5

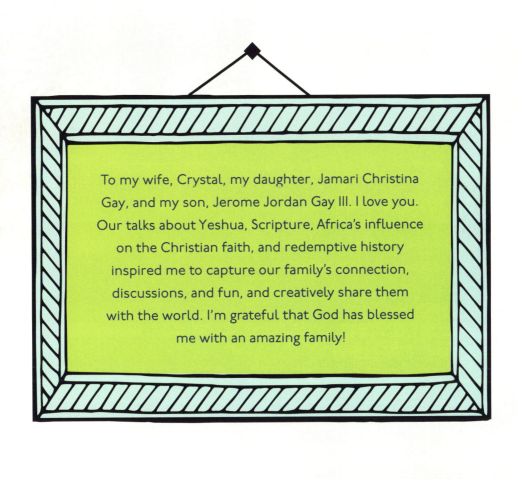

To my wife, Crystal, my daughter, Jamari Christina Gay, and my son, Jerome Jordan Gay III. I love you. Our talks about Yeshua, Scripture, Africa's influence on the Christian faith, and redemptive history inspired me to capture our family's connection, discussions, and fun, and creatively share them with the world. I'm grateful that God has blessed me with an amazing family!

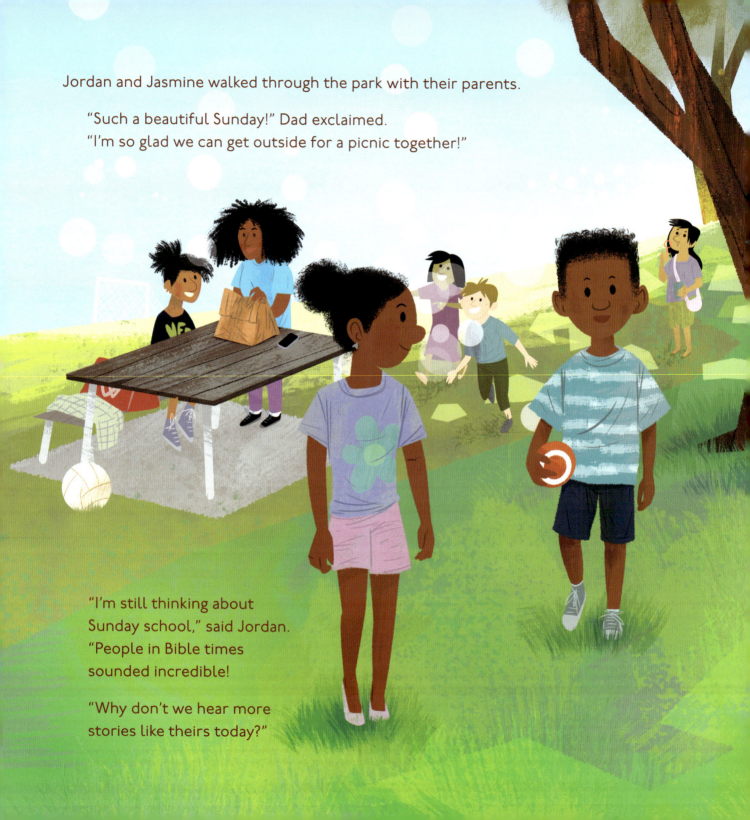

Jordan and Jasmine walked through the park with their parents.

"Such a beautiful Sunday!" Dad exclaimed.
"I'm so glad we can get outside for a picnic together!"

"I'm still thinking about Sunday school," said Jordan. "People in Bible times sounded incredible!

"Why don't we hear more stories like theirs today?"

"I can think
of similar stories
from history,"
said Dad.

"Of real people?" Jordan exclaimed.
"What did they do? Where were they from?"

Dad replied, "There are many heroes of the faith—
and remarkable theologians—many from Africa."

"What's a theologian?" asked Jasmine.

"A theologian is a person who studies about God," said Mom.
"They study to know him better and to share him with others."

"Can we hear their stories?" asked Jordan.

"Sure. Let's start with some people who lived a long, long time ago,
when the good news of Jesus was just starting to spread around the world,"
said Dad. "They lived back when the Christian faith was almost brand new."

"Remember your leaders. They spoke God's word to you. Think about the results of their way of life. Copy their faith."

HEBREWS 13:7

Tertullian

A boy named Tertullian grew up in the city of Carthage—a prosperous, busy, port city in Tunisia. His father was an officer in an African-based army. Because his father had great power in Rome, Tertullian was able to attend the very best schools (in Carthage)—all the way through college! That's when he became a lawyer.

It wasn't until Tertullian was in his twenties, that he became a follower of Jesus and began writing stories about God. He was the first author to write Christian books in the Latin language. And he also wrote several books in Greek.

Have you ever heard the word, Trinity? Tertullian penned it! Trinity means: God is one God, but he has three persons—the Father, the Son, and the Holy Spirit. Although you might see this idea in the Bible, Tertullian was the first person to give it a name!

When you read your Bible, you also might notice how it's divided into two big parts. Tertullian created these parts called the Old and New Testaments. The Old Testament has thirty-nine books, and the New Testament has twenty-seven! That's a lot of books!

Tertullian loved to stand up for God's Word. If he ever heard anyone making fun of God, or spreading lies about him, he quickly ran to God's defense. He didn't want anyone believing things about God that weren't true.

Tertullian spent over twenty years writing about God and sharing him with others. He even defended the Bible before the Roman Empire! He was brave, wise, and displayed great leadership.

"Lead a life of love, just as Christ did. He loved us. He gave himself up for us.
He was a sweet-smelling offering and sacrifice to God."

EPHESIANS 5:2

Perpetua + Felicity

There once lived two friends who were as close as sisters. Their names were Perpetua and Felicity. They lived in Carthage, just like Tertullian, and they loved Jesus deeply.

Perpetua was a noblewoman from a very important family. And Felicity came to know Jesus through her. Together, they shared their faith with anyone who would listen.

During that time, there was an emperor who wanted to be the most powerful ruler in all the world! So, when he heard that people were following after Jesus, and sharing his message with others, he felt threatened—and angry.

When Perpetua was about twenty-two years old, the emperor arrested her and Felicity and sent them to jail. He thought that would silence their message, but he was wrong.

While in prison, Perpetua's father visited her three times.

Each time, he begged her to stop following Jesus, and each time, Perpetua refused. She continued sharing God's message, even with the prison guards, and some believed!

Each day in prison, Perpetua wrote in a diary. This is how we have her story today! She wrote that no matter what happened to her and Felicity, Jesus would always be with them. Often, late at night, while Perpetua was sleeping, God would meet her in wonderful dreams. She felt such comfort!

One day, prison guards took Perpetua and Felicity and killed them. When someone dies because of their faith, we say they are martyred. Even as they faced death, these two friends, who were true sisters in Christ, bravely lived and died with sacrifice and passion.

"The Lᴏʀᴅ looks out over the whole earth. He gives strength to those who commit their lives completely to him."

2 CHRONICLES 16:9a

Origen of Alexandria

A boy named Origen grew up in the city of Alexandria in Egypt. His parents loved Jesus and faithfully taught their nine children about God. Origen, who was the oldest, memorized many, many Bible verses. Even as a child, he thought about God all the time and asked his parents many hard questions about the Bible.

People who loved Jesus had a hard time in Origen's day. When his father was put into jail for believing in Jesus, Origen wanted to go too—but he was too young. His mother encouraged him to continue telling others about Jesus—just like his father had done.

When Origen grew up, one of his favorite things was to write stories
about God. Each day, Origen wrote more and more stories,
so that by the end of his life, he had written nearly 6,000!

(Just imagine how long it would take to read all those stories!
And how many shelves it would take to hold them all!)
Many of Origen's writings explain how to understand the Bible.

Because Origen had a strong commitment to helping people read and understand God's Word, he spent each day helping answer their questions. He helped them understand the Bible's message and teaching. And he shared many stories so that they could remember them and share God's Word with others.

"Some trust in chariots. Some trust in horses.
But we trust in the LORD our God."

PSALM 20:7

Cyprian of Carthage

In addition to Carthage being the home of Tertullian, Perpetua, and Felicity, it was also the home of another leader named Cyprian. Though his parents were not believers, he came to know Jesus as he grew older. He even opened a school of his own to teach people about God!

From the moment Cyprian began following Jesus, he shared God's message with anyone who would listen. He spent each day writing stories about God—so that his message would spread far and wide.

But one day, when Cyprian was working as a bishop, or church leader, he received some troubling news. (If you've ever encountered a bully—or met someone who makes your life

difficult—you'll relate to this part of the story.) You see, there was a powerful emperor named Decius. He hated Cyprian for being a follower of Jesus. So, he decided to chase after Cyprian—and make his life difficult—for as long as it would take for Cyprian to stop sharing about Jesus.

At first, Cyprian wondered what he should do. If he continued sharing, the emperor would surely find him! But staying silent didn't seem right, either. Cyprian prayed for help, and God gave him confidence. The Lord helped him to remember that his Word was true no matter what the emperor thought. God promised to always be with him and help him.

So, Cyprian continued writing letters to the church, and his words spread far and wide. His confidence in the Lord became contagious, and the church trusted God's Word.

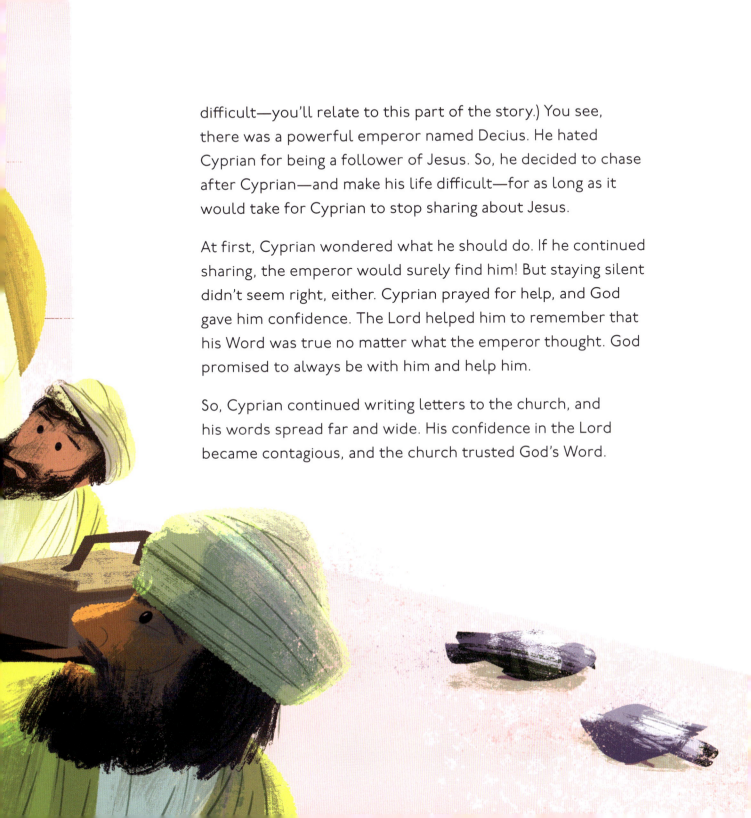

"We all have gifts. They differ according to the grace God has given to each of us . . . Use [your gifts] according to the faith you have."

ROMANS 12:6

Lactantius

L actantius lived in North Africa. He was a gifted author and teacher. He was even appointed as a teacher for the emperor!

God gave Lactantius a wonderful gift: creativity. (Are you creative? Do you ever use your imagination to play out stories? Or write songs? Maybe you like to build, or draw, or paint? There are many ways to be creative!) Lactantius was creative in his writing and teaching. He quickly became one of North Africa's favorite Christian authors and teachers.

More than anything, Lactantius wanted God's people to understand the Bible. In that day many people were spreading lies about God. Lactantius wanted believers to understand God's Word so well, that they could easily tell the truth from a lie.

One day, when Lactantius was busy at work, he saw something terribly sad. He saw the emperor pestering Christians and treating them poorly. In that moment, Lactantius decided to quit his job teaching for the emperor. But he continued teaching for God.

Lactantius reminds us that God gives each of his followers special gifts to honor him. What gifts has he given you? How can you use them to praise him?

"Dear children, don't just talk about love.
Put your love into action. Then it will truly be love."

1 JOHN 3:18

Pachomius the Great

T here once lived a man named Pachomius the Great. As a young child growing up in Thebes, Egypt, he never heard about God. But as he grew up, God met Pachomius in a special way.

When Pachomius was about twenty-two years old, Roman soldiers pounded on his front door, dragged him out into the street, and forced him to join their army. Pachomius didn't like wars or fighting, but he had no choice in the matter.

One day, when he and the other soldiers were weak and hungry, neighbors brought food to them. Another day, when they were wet and cold, the neighbors brought blankets. When soldiers were hurt in battle, the neighbors healed their wounds. When

Pachomius learned that those helpful, caring neighbors were Christians, he grew curious about their God.

Then Pachomius witnessed something upsetting. He watched the emperor persecute, or poorly treat, the Christians for their faith. (Do you remember the names of the two friends who were treated poorly for their faith?)

When Pachomius saw what was happening—and how the Christians didn't fight back, but instead responded with love—Pachomius was stunned! He was so moved by their love, that he decided to follow Jesus himself!

Through the years, as Pachomius grew closer to Jesus, he often sought quiet places where he could pray to God. Because he enjoyed this so much, he decided to create a place where other Christians could do the same.

Pachomius started a community where believers could live together, worship God, and help their neighbors. By the time Pachomius died, he had created eight communities with several hundred people!

"Be strong and brave. Do not be afraid. Do not lose hope.
I am the LORD your God. I will be with you everywhere you go."

JOSHUA 1:9

Athanasius

One morning in the bustling city of Alexandria, Egypt, Bishop Alexander looked toward the seaside. There on the beach, he noticed a group of young boys playing together. One boy, Athanasius, was pretending to baptize the other boys. When the bishop met the boys and heard of their love for God, he began teaching them the Bible.

With each passing year, Athanasius grew in his love for God. He loved thinking about God, and writing about God, and telling everyone he could about God.

So, when he heard that a man in Alexandria was spreading

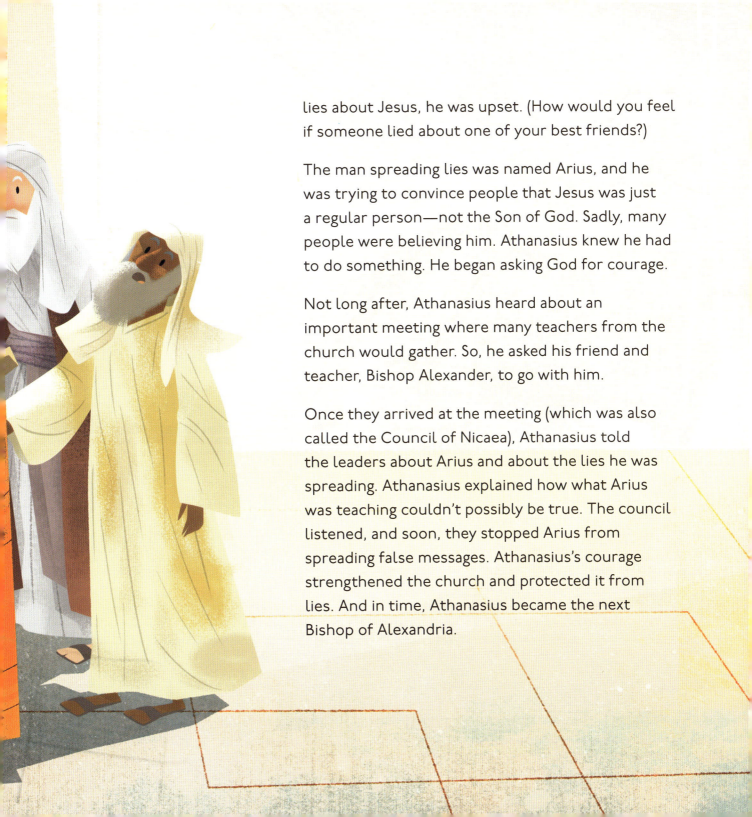

lies about Jesus, he was upset. (How would you feel if someone lied about one of your best friends?)

The man spreading lies was named Arius, and he was trying to convince people that Jesus was just a regular person—not the Son of God. Sadly, many people were believing him. Athanasius knew he had to do something. He began asking God for courage.

Not long after, Athanasius heard about an important meeting where many teachers from the church would gather. So, he asked his friend and teacher, Bishop Alexander, to go with him.

Once they arrived at the meeting (which was also called the Council of Nicaea), Athanasius told the leaders about Arius and about the lies he was spreading. Athanasius explained how what Arius was teaching couldn't possibly be true. The council listened, and soon, they stopped Arius from spreading false messages. Athanasius's courage strengthened the church and protected it from lies. And in time, Athanasius became the next Bishop of Alexandria.

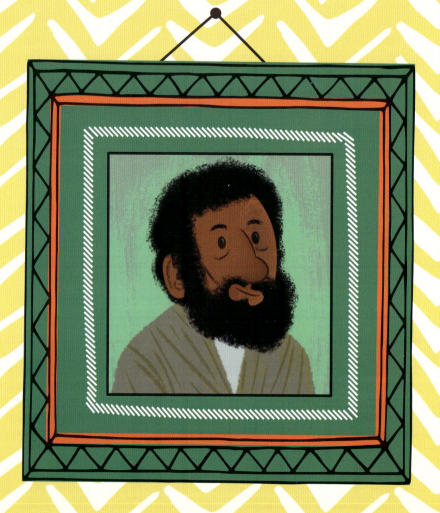

"Love one another deeply. Honor others more than yourselves."

ROMANS 12:10

Shenoute of Atripe

O ne day in the country of Egypt, an elderly man was near the end of his life. He loved his young nephew Shenoute and wanted to share something special with him. He wanted to give him an inheritance—a treasure to keep and remember him by. Some people inherit money or objects, while others inherit nothing at all. But this uncle decided to give his nephew something extra special: the monastery he had started in Atripe. (Remember Pachomius and his community? A monastery is a place where people live, worship, and serve God together.)

Shenoute had grown up in the monastery. It was his home. And as he grew into a man, he cared for it and became its leader. He was also a leader at church.

Together, the people of Shenoute's monastery worked, prayed, and obeyed God. Shenoute taught them the Bible and together, they cared for the poor in their community.

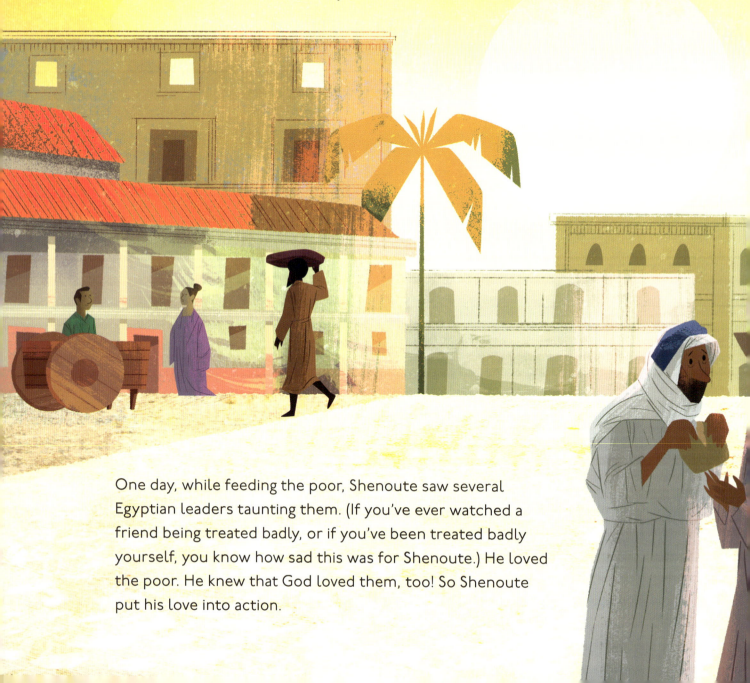

One day, while feeding the poor, Shenoute saw several Egyptian leaders taunting them. (If you've ever watched a friend being treated badly, or if you've been treated badly yourself, you know how sad this was for Shenoute.) He loved the poor. He knew that God loved them, too! So Shenoute put his love into action.

Shenoute walked up to the Egyptian leaders bravely but respectfully and stood up for his friends. He lived out the Bible verse that says, "Dear children, don't just talk about love. Put your love into action. Then it will truly be love" (1 John 3:18).

For the rest of his life, Shenoute of Atripe continued to stand for the rights of the poor. He hoped that one day, all people would be treated with the same love and respect.

"God's grace has saved you because of your faith in Christ. Your salvation doesn't come from anything you do. It is God's gift."

EPHESIANS 2:8

Augustine

I n Thagaste, Algeria, lived a young boy who loved getting into mischief. He loved playing pranks and impressing his friends. One day, he stole pears from a neighbor's tree. When he was too full to finish eating them, he threw them to a group of pigs. The boy's name was Augustine.

Augustine's mother, Monica, loved God, and each night before bed, she told him stories about God's grace. She always prayed that one day he would follow Jesus. But Augustine wasn't interested in her stories or in Jesus.

With each passing year, Monica continued praying for her son, and her prayers followed him everywhere he went.

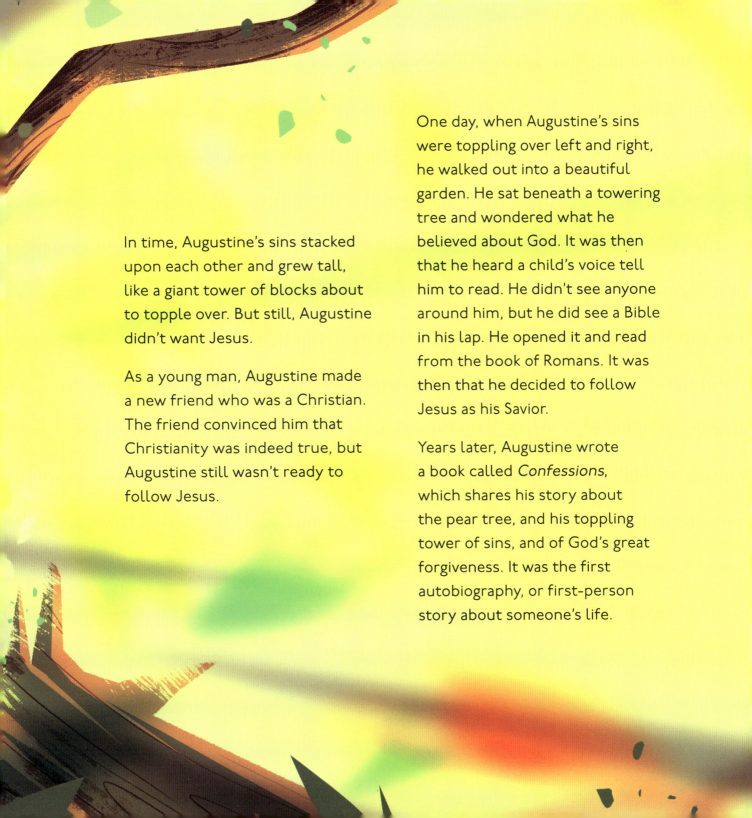

In time, Augustine's sins stacked upon each other and grew tall, like a giant tower of blocks about to topple over. But still, Augustine didn't want Jesus.

As a young man, Augustine made a new friend who was a Christian. The friend convinced him that Christianity was indeed true, but Augustine still wasn't ready to follow Jesus.

One day, when Augustine's sins were toppling over left and right, he walked out into a beautiful garden. He sat beneath a towering tree and wondered what he believed about God. It was then that he heard a child's voice tell him to read. He didn't see anyone around him, but he did see a Bible in his lap. He opened it and read from the book of Romans. It was then that he decided to follow Jesus as his Savior.

Years later, Augustine wrote a book called *Confessions*, which shares his story about the pear tree, and his toppling tower of sins, and of God's great forgiveness. It was the first autobiography, or first-person story about someone's life.

"When you hope, be joyful. When you suffer, be patient. When you pray, be faithful."

ROMANS 12:12

Cyril of Alexandria

Many years ago, in a place called Didouseya, Egypt, lived a man who loved sharing the good news of Jesus. His name was Cyril, and more than anything, he wanted others to know his Savior.

Cyril had grown up in a family who loved God. His own uncle was the Patriarch of Alexandria—or head of the church. But more than serving the church, Cyril wanted to share God's Word with those who had never heard it. He wanted to be a missionary. A missionary is someone who goes out to share the good news of Jesus. (Do you know any missionaries? Where do they live? What do they do?)

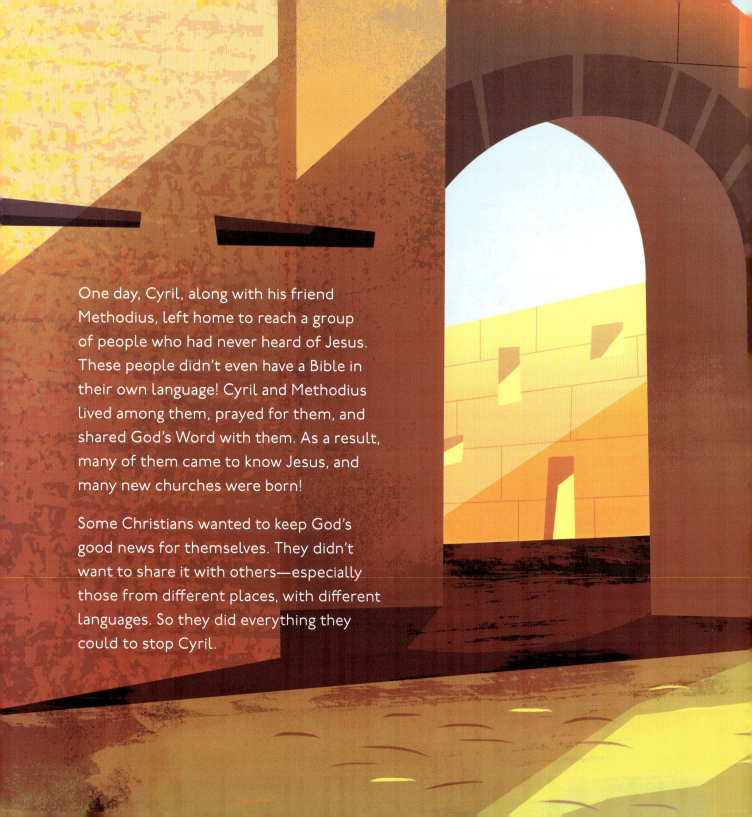

One day, Cyril, along with his friend Methodius, left home to reach a group of people who had never heard of Jesus. These people didn't even have a Bible in their own language! Cyril and Methodius lived among them, prayed for them, and shared God's Word with them. As a result, many of them came to know Jesus, and many new churches were born!

Some Christians wanted to keep God's good news for themselves. They didn't want to share it with others—especially those from different places, with different languages. So they did everything they could to stop Cyril.

But God gave Cyril strength, and he did not give up! He continued sharing the gospel with determination. And one day, God set Cyril in a place of honor. He became the Patriarch of Alexandria—just like his uncle—where he continued spreading God's good news all over the world.

Jordan and Jasmine sat in awe as their parents
finished sharing the stories of God's African heroes.

"And this is just the beginning," marveled Dad.
"There are many more stories to tell!"

Mom continued, "What's amazing is that all
these stories wouldn't exist without Jesus. Nothing
compares to the true story of our God and Savior,
who lived, died, and rose again, for our salvation.
He's the reason all these heroes and legacies exist!"

"That's right!" exclaimed Jordan.
"They were following after Jesus!"

Jasmine reflected, "I hope one day,
we'll have our own stories and legacies to share."

"We pray so—and we believe you will!"
exclaimed Dad and Mom together.

HALL OF HEROES

TERTULLIAN
LEADERSHIP
C. 155 AD – C. 220 AD

ORIGEN OF ALEXANDRIA
COMMITMENT
C. 185 AD – C. 254 AD

PERPETUA

SACRIFICE + PASSION

C. 182 AD – C. 203 AD

FELICITY

SACRIFICE + PASSION

C. 182 AD – C. 203 AD

ATHANASIUS

COURAGE

C. 293 AD – C. 373 AD

CYPRIAN OF CARTHAGE
CONFIDENCE
C. 200 AD – C. 258 AD

LACTANTIUS
CREATIVITY
C. 250 AD – C. 325 AD

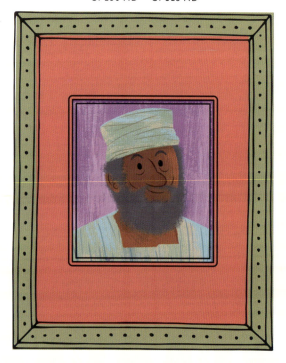

PACHOMIUS THE GREAT
SERVICE
C. 290 AD – C. 346 AD

CYRIL OF ALEXANDRIA

DETERMINATION

C. 375 AD – C. 444 AD

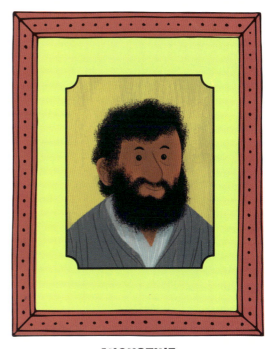

AUGUSTINE

GRACE

C. 354 AD – C. 430 AD

SHENOUTE OF ATRIPE

LOVE

C. 350 AD – C. 466 AD

And most certainly, the mystery of godliness is great: [Jesus] was manifested in the flesh, vindicated in the Spirit, seen by angels, preached among the nations, believed on in the world, taken up in glory.

I TIMOTHY 3:16 CSB

Acknowledgments

I'm grateful to Dan, Barbara, and everyone at New
Growth Press. To John, for illustrating and capturing
the beautiful contributions of African theologians,
philosophers, and martyrs in a way that children can
understand and engage with. To my mom and brother
for your constant love and encouragement. To everyone
at Vision Church for your love and support. Thanks
to everyone listed and quite a few missing who have
made this possible. I'm grateful for each of you.

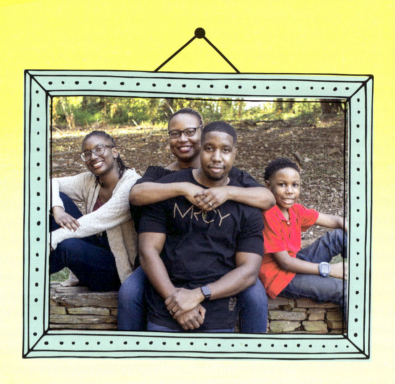

Author's Note

I wrote this book to inspire families—and children, especially—with the beautiful mosaic of Christianity and its history. Africa's contribution to Christianity, and the people God used in his plan, are not often highlighted in a way that reflects the beautiful diversity of people in antiquity. I wanted to provide a resource where children can be inspired by people God has used for his glory and see themselves as part of God's plan going forward. I hope you'll be inspired by the characteristics displayed in each African hero, and compelled to teach your children a history of our faith that includes people of all hues.